a FORK *in the* ROAD

a FORK *in the* ROAD

MODERN ESTATE PLANNING & HOW ELDER LAW IS TAKING THE OTHER FORK

Jeffrey R. Bellomo, Daniel D. Hill

Published by Best Seller Publishing®, St. Augustine, FL
Best Seller Publishing® is a registered trademark.
Printed in the United States of America.
ISBN:978-1-959840-82-4

For more information, please write:
Best Seller Publishing®
53 Marine Street
St. Augustine, FL 32084
or call 1 (626) 765-9750
Visit us online at: www.BestSellerPublishing.org

Contents

Part III: After-Death Asset Protection (How It All Comes Together)

Preface

My name is Jeffrey Bellomo, and I am an estate planning and elder law attorney in Pennsylvania. I am passionate about what I do and have been practicing for approximately 20 years! In this book, I'll be relating what happened to Bob and Sally's family. But my own family also had some difficult times. My sole purpose and motivation is to ensure that all families are educated about estate planning and elder law so that what happened to my family in the hospital room does not happen to any of yours.

My family was unfortunate in that my mother was ill and we were told that she might need different levels of care, possibly including in-home care, assisted living, hospice, or skilled care (nursing home eligible). At that point in time, we were not educated and had a ton of questions like these: *Will Dad lose the house? Is there anything that can be done in crisis? Should we have done stuff sooner?*

The cancer was very bad. The doctor was very confident in his abilities as a surgeon but feared that Mom would not come out of surgery without needing additional care. He told us to seek the advice of an attorney to get the answers we needed, as he foresaw that we would require help. So, we met with two different attorneys, and the only thing they told us was that it cost $300 just to meet with the attorney, and if we wanted the plan or solution to protect the family assets, the fee would be $15,000. If we hired the law firm in that moment, they would roll the $300 into the planning fee. However, if we set foot out of the office, we would forfeit our $300.

We walked out of the office and allowed them to keep the $300 because there was no way we were going to spend money without knowing who the estate planner was, whether we could trust them, or even anything about what the plan was and how it would work. The lawyers were very vague in the meeting and would not provide detailed answers to questions. They refused to walk us through the plan or explain what they would be doing for our family. I promised my family that day that I would not allow this to happen in the future to other families. The truth is, during times when a loved one is ill, the last thing you want your family to go through is being taken advantage of financially. As you can imagine, families are having to deal with enough challenges during times of crisis.

This ordeal with my mom in the hospital happened two weeks before the bar exam. I was able to take the bar exam and pass, and then I clerked in the Lancaster Court of Common Pleas for Judge David L. Ashworth. I was fortunate to get a job right after my clerkship for a firm in York, Pennsylvania. Ours was a general practice law firm. I did not like being a jack of all trades and master of none. I went to another firm and did solely business and estate planning work.

After working in other law firms for several years, I realized that I had become one of many law firm associates obligated to do what the partners tell you to do and charge the way that their practices indicate. I decided that it was time to make a change.

Not only did I want to change my practice, I was hopeful to change the industry. I joined an organization called Lawyers with Purpose® and learned a model that was education-based, first and foremost. This means a family can attend a workshop (a workshop is a small group of people in a room getting educated on estate planning and elder law for about two hours); they will then receive a free consultation. I absolutely fell in love with the model, as it was everything that I believed in, something I would create for my own firm and use in the future. I've been with Lawyers with Purpose® for over 13 years now and continue to offer free workshops in estate planning, crisis planning, special needs planning, probate administration, and trust administration. My entire focus is to help clients so that what happened to my family does not happen to yours.

The co-author of this book is attorney Dan Hill. Dan and I were law school study partners and helped get each other through our very tough law school years. Law school stretched us both to the brink, with the hours of studying and final exams. Dan and I are currently attorneys with *Bellomo and Associates*. We had been discussing writing a book since our days together on the law review, and now that we have been working together for over three years, we hope in this way to give back to our community and to grow it into something bigger and better. Dan is one of the smartest and kindest human beings I know. He has been integral in helping me with this book and allowing me to write it. (He is taking meetings with clients for me so that I can focus on this book and other tasks.)

We were very good throughout our careers, practicing and preserving wealth and assets for families. We were able to protect clients' assets, not only during their lifetimes but also after death. In my first job out of law school, I worked with an attorney who helped disbar several lawyers who were running a scheme against the elderly. Their con involved an unethical ploy where they would send out insurance agents to meet with prospects, to sell revocable living trusts. The attorneys would never fund the trusts, and those trusts were absolutely useless.

Because of that experience, I had assumed that all revocable trusts were bad. Once I started understanding trusts in detail, I realized it was not the trusts that were bad but rather these unethical attorneys who were doing them and not properly funding them. I have had a great run for almost 20 years where we were able to do asset protection after death in a testamentary trust—a trust in a will. So in my mind, all revocable trusts were bad, and in my heart wills were cheaper (at least the upfront costs were less).

Over the last six months, we have now come upon a minimum of seven financial firms that will not allow beneficiary designation to occur in a testamentary trust and in a will. These firms are all indicating to us they want theirs to be a living trust, whether revocable or irrevocable; they just want it to be a trust that is in existence now during life and that does not have to wait until a death occurs. We did not know why they took this position and did not understand the benefit to them by taking this stance. We spent countless hours trying to change this and trying to come up with a plan B, to no avail.

In one recent conversation I had with a company's Legal Counsel, I asked, "What do you want me to do and how do you want me to proceed moving forward?" The response of the attorney for the financial institution was like that of everyone else. He said, "Just do a living trust and be done with it already." I had tried for years to avoid using a living trust because of my prior experience, but now I'm willing to admit I was wrong and that I see the value of a living trust for clients.

This has certainly been a tough journey for me: to admit that I was wrong. (Not all trusts are bad. My previous experiences were with companies that did not use them correctly and used and abused them to make a profit.) Now that these current clients' financial companies are forcing my hand and will not allow me to use the testamentary trust, we have no choice. Asset protection after death for the benefit of our clients' children is way too important to not do simply because financial companies are throwing up a roadblock.

We are currently using revocable living trusts in place of what used to be our testamentary trust, to serve the purpose of asset protection after death. We have been helping families move forward using a revocable trust for all assets for which the client is not seeking asset protection. By doing this, we are typically saving families a lot of money on the back end, because the fee to administer a trust is 2% versus the standard sliding scale, which often works out to approximately 5%.

While the family may pay a little bit more on the front end to do a trust, again, it certainly saves them tons of money on the back end. In this way, we not only avoid probate in all the states where the individual may own property, but we also are able to achieve asset protection after death for all of the beneficiaries. We are able to protect assets for people who have special needs, for individuals who are spendthrifts or addicts, as well as for individuals who simply do not want to see their assets lost to a divorce, nursing home, or car accident. The revocable trust affords us this ability.

We also used an irrevocable pure grantor asset protection trust® (IPUG®) as a way to protect assets from long-term care costs. And because such a trust is still under the control of the grantor (the grantor is the person who created the trust), we are able to pay the Pennsylvania inheritance tax at the applicable rate to receive a step-up in basis on the value of the grantor's property on the date of death of the decedent grantor. First, let me explain the term "basis": it is what the person paid for the asset. When a person receives property at death, this means that the person receiving the property gets the basis on the date of death, rather than the basis the person had in it when he or she bought the item.

This allows the beneficiaries to receive a step-up in basis and avoid a huge capital gains implication. Capital gains tax is assessed on the person who sells the property. If the person received the asset at death, then they received the step-up in basis and would only pay capital gains tax from the date of death value to what they sold the asset for. However, if they were gifted the asset during life, they would pay capital gains tax from the basis that the original owner had in the property to the date of sale, based on current capital gains tax schedules.

It is the best of all worlds, since they are able to get asset protection during life but also a step-up in basis to where the beneficiaries are protected under the current law. We use the *two trusts (revocable trust and irrevocable grantor trust)* in tandem to be able to avoid probate for all assets while protecting these during life for assets other than retirement accounts.

FOREWORD

by David J. Zumpano, Esq.

I have known Jeff Bellomo since 2009, when I met him at a national estate planning conference for lawyers. I remember thinking, "This guy is different; he leads with his heart!" He had all the accreditations that showed his intelligence, an L.L.M. in Tax, his CELA (Certification as an Elder Law Attorney, which fewer than 200 attorneys in the country had at the time), and he was really kind, something attorneys are not traditionally known for. What was surprising to me was, he was struggling to have a successful practice. This was contradictory; he had everything he needed to succeed but didn't know how to apply it. Truth is, law school doesn't teach how to run a law practice; it just teaches how to take a position on the law so that you can advocate for your client.

In this book, you will take Jeff's journey with him from when he started as a client looking for guidance after his mom's health took an unexpected turn for the worse to where he is today, the leader of a law firm that has empowered many thousands of clients to be informed and to create estate plans that keep them in control when the unexpected happens. Jeff's heart would never let the experience he had happen to another family, and his intelligence ensures that everyday folks can stay one step ahead of the tragedy they never expect.

It was fate we met that day. I was once like Jeff, but I was a CPA and attorney and, unlike Jeff, grew up in a family of entrepreneurs. In fact, by the time we met, I had founded a national organization for estate planning and asset protection lawyers to help them build a practice that shares their knowledge in a way consumers prefer, rather than the traditional approach most lawyers use. (Let's face it, no one wakes up and says, "It's a great day to go see a lawyer.") Jeff focuses on educating consumers, and the other professionals they work with, on what he sees every day in his office and how they can avoid the complexities that happen and ensure control stays within their families, not the lawyers and courts. Jeff quickly learned how being the kind person he is does not have to conflict with his intelligence and how he can share his passion with his clients so that they never have the experience he had with his mother.

Jeff is a lifetime learner, and after joining my national legal organization, Lawyers with Purpose®, quickly became a star student and an attorney admired by other attorneys across the country. He is so passionate about what he does that he wanted to make sure other attorneys across the United States protected families in their areas like he was committed to doing in the York, Pennsylvania, area. So Jeff began training to pass on his knowledge and passion to all new members. He always stays on top of the most cutting-edge planning techniques and strategies used nationwide. He is an incredible speaker and, as you will see from this book, a great author as well. He continues to coach attorneys and their team members across the country on best practices to create the most value for consumers and the other professionals they work with.

A core principle Jeff adopted is the importance of working with the other professionals who work with his clients. This ensures the ultimate goals of the client are achieved. Jeff knows what he is capable of, but he must rely on his clients' accountants, bankers, financial professionals, and health care providers to ensure all are aligned with the legal plan he creates for his clients. Jeff is leading the industry to change the landscape from the traditional model of planning to a new model, shaping the future of estate planning, as illustrated in the techniques he describes in this book.

Jeff is beyond qualified to write about asset protection during life and after death, and in addition to his vast knowledge and passion, he is open, curious, aware, collaborative, adaptable, and generous. In this book, Jeff lives these core values by bringing to life real fact patterns in cases that occur every day. He never says no, or can't, but rather asks *Why?*, or *How can we … ?* Jeff is the first to assist individuals or organizations that can impact his clients and community without any expectation of reciprocity and is genuinely interested in others' ideas and thoughts. He asks questions to seek information from all he encounters to continue to discover ways to improve beyond his current knowledge and accepts change is inherent in growth.

Jeff and his entire team at Bellomo and Associates embrace the change necessary to move others and their community forward. He is always growing and looking for ways to make himself, his team, other professionals, and the community better. He is full of "wonder" and uses the skills he teaches our lawyers across the country to discover what he didn't know, and those engaging with him feel heard. In this book, you will experience wonder and feel like he has connected with you in ways you didn't know mattered to you.

Jeff always remains present to behaviors that inhibit progress and helps identify others' gifts that simplify the path to success by utilizing his and others unique talents to create the most effective solutions to achieve the desired outcome. Who Jeff is will become more apparent as you read the real-life stories (and more importantly, the solutions) he shares. He truly celebrates and loves everyone he encounters and keeps his commitments. Working with Jeff ensures you never experience the helplessness he felt when facing his mother's crisis.

What's even more exciting is that he has built a law firm of over twenty individuals who share and exhibit his core values. Together, they use their talents and resources with one another, their clients, allied professionals, and the York community. They are always available to help you (yes, you who are reading this book) with education, resources, and solutions that are not commonly available and do so by following a trusted and true process that ensures each client's individual needs are identified and provided for. Interestingly, Jeff coined the phrase in 2012 at Lawyers with Purpose to FDS™, or follow the darn system. It allows him to help more people by offering more solutions and more support than typically available.

You are about to take a journey few people take prior to having to. This book will enable you to become empowered to achieve things not previously considered and to ensure you never become one of the stories he shares. More importantly, you will come to know the relevance of the term "estate planning" we all hear about but never fully understand and will be willing to proactively engage in it (it truly is the greatest gift you can give yourself and your loved ones!) Let your education begin by being guided by one of the smartest, kindest, most genuine individuals to share on your personal journey. He has and continues to inspire me and hundreds of attorneys across the country with his knowledge, passion, and leadership to provide cutting-edge solutions to avoid common, everyday challenges. I am excited he gets to share it now with you.

David J. Zumpano, Esq.
March 2023

Introduction

Bob and Sally were like many other married couples in York, Pennsylvania. They worked incredibly hard their entire lives to provide for themselves and their family. Unfortunately, Bob's family lost a majority of their assets to long-term care costs (his mother was in a nursing home for an extended period of time), and he vowed not to let that happen to his family.

Bob and Sally were very well read and knew how easy it was for children to lose their inheritance to their spouses, accidents, long-term care costs, other creditors, and predators. Like most of our clients, they did not want that to happen to their family. Bob and Sally used the reputable Attorney Smidge in town and had done so for a long time. In fact, they met Attorney Smidge through Bob's parents who used him 30 plus years ago for a real estate closing.

Bob and Sally had three children, who we will refer to as Mark, James, and Kyle. All three were very good kids. Bob and Sally loved all of them. Mark was the oldest and most responsible. His marriage was okay, but he and his wife had their moments. It wasn't all roses, but overall, they did their best and loved each other most days.

James had special needs. He was receiving public benefits from the government and needed them for his housing and income. He would be in trouble if he ever lost his benefits.

Kyle was a good kid. He simply had not grown up and at times made decisions that were questionable at best.

Mark had children of his own, Dan, Jeff, and Reese—whose experiences will be covered in Part III of this book. Dan is much like his father. Overall, a great person. However, Dan's marriage can be an issue at times. Mark often looks at his son and sees a reflection of himself and his own marriage.

Jeff has special needs. He is dependent on his government benefits for housing and income.

And Reese is finding his way. Every now and then he drinks too much, and it can lead to a rash of unfortunate decisions.

The family had a very tight bond. They respectfully followed the lead of Bob and Sally, but Bob was the strong head of the family who was seen with deep reverence by all members. Bob had made it very clear that he wanted to protect what he worked so hard for from long-term care costs, including protecting his children from their spouses along with creditors and predators.

They were a very common family in terms of assets and desires. Bob and Sally had worked very hard during their lives. They had a house and other assets totaling just shy of $2.5 million, and they did not want to see them lost to nursing homes or by their children's creditors and predators.

PART I

Solvable Problems
(The Dangers of Old Traditions)

Chapter One

The Challenge of Estate Planning: Now's the Time for Elder Law

SEEKING LEGAL ADVICE FROM ATTORNEY SMIDGE

"Attorney Smidge, my name is Bob Jones, and this is my wife, Sally. We are very excited to meet you and look forward to working with you and your firm. You all come very highly recommended." I was a little surprised when we walked into Attorney Smidge's office to learn that he was the only attorney in his firm and there were no predecessors. I was also surprised to see several client questionnaires for family law matters and an advertisement for his criminal law practice as well as his website, which called him a general practice attorney.

Attorney Smidge replied and asked, "Hi Bob and Sally, pleased to meet you. What brings you into the office and what could I help you with?"

"It is very important to us that we protect our assets in case one of us ever needed long-term care and also to ensure that our three children would be protected if anything were to happen to us," replied Bob.

Attorney Smidge looked puzzled and asked Bob, "What are you concerned about? You have almost a million and a half dollars."

Bob explained, "I worked very hard for that money and missed out on a lot of my children's events and schooling, all because I believed that it was what was best for my family, not only while we are alive but after Sally and I die to make sure that the kids are taken care of. I want to ensure that what we worked very hard to accumulate does not get lost in a matter of a few months because of long-term care costs. I cannot qualify for long-term care insurance, and although Sally can, it is so cost-prohibitive that we would not be able to live comfortably and would be insurance poor." He continued, "I watched my parents lose a ton of assets for long-term care and do not want that to happen to me or my children."

Attorney Smidge looked taken aback and perplexed and said, "Who do you expect to pay for your care, then?"

OLD TRADITIONS & CONVENTIONS

Estate Planning

Traditionally, most estate planning attorneys tend to believe that planning can be accomplished by simply providing people with a last will and testament, a financial power of attorney, and a medical power of attorney. The belief is that whatever happens during one's lifetime to their assets was intended to happen, and if a person loses the money to a nursing home, well, so be it. A traditional estate planning attorney also tends to believe that after death, the assets should be provided outright to the beneficiaries. The phrase that is often heard in the estate planning context is that *you do not want to control from the grave.* I have always said, and truly believe, that nobody wants to control from the grave but that everybody would like to protect from the grave.

Financial Advising

Many financial advisors and insurance agents often urge their clients to beneficiary designate all assets to avoid probate (probate is the legal process by which we carry out your wishes in your will after you pass) and to ward off attorneys and costs. The problem with this logic is that the assets must go outright to the beneficiaries. When this happens, the assets are now subject to the creditors and predators in the beneficiary's life. Once an asset goes outright, there is no way to protect it for or from the following:

- The spouse
- Future spouses
- Long-term costs
- The children (their potential divorces, car accidents, and long-term care costs)

Federal Estate Tax Planning Using Trusts

To the extent that an estate planning attorney does federal estate tax planning, their practice areas will force them or encourage them to do higher-end planning using trusts. However, in this context, they are using a trust to reduce the federal estate tax money that is owed to the federal government. Currently, the federal estate tax limit is $12.92 million a person, which is doubled for a married couple. Very few individuals in the country actually have a federal estate tax problem presently. Therefore, most of those estate planning techniques are not currently being used.

In 2025, the law is set to come back to $5 million a person plus inflation, which we believe will be around $5.8 million, or $11.6 million per couple. This means that people in 2025 with less than $5.8 million a person will not pay federal estate tax. Although we may see an increase in tax planning, this type of planning is not specifically what an elder law attorney uses for one or two main reasons. First of all, in the context of elder law, we don't care if the money is out of the estate. In fact, we want the money to be included in the estate of the person who we are doing the planning for because we want to step-up in basis on the value of the assets. If a person is gifted assets during life, their basis is considered a carryover basis—meaning the person is gifting the money for the asset. If the person dies with the asset in their name or in a trust that they control, the receiver receives the basis on the date of death. The Fair Market Value (FMV) is determined by what the asset is worth on the date of death. The receiver then only pays capital gains tax on the difference.

Most tax attorneys are looking to get the money out of the person's estate. Therefore, they do not receive a step-up in basis, and the children will be responsible for significant capital gains taxes.

Secondly, in the context of elder law, most clients have modest wealth of a couple hundred thousand dollars to several million, but certainly nowhere near the federal estate tax exemption amounts. Even if the exemption amounts come back to 5.8 million per person, there still will not be a large percentage of people with an issue. Elder law and asset protection is more common and arguably more needed for people in the range of $250,000–$3 million in assets (people with more than that believe they can self-fund for their long-term care costs).

DON'T GET LEFT BEHIND USING TRADITIONAL ESTATE PLANNING

Traditional estate planning attorneys typically shy away from some of the techniques of the elder law attorney bar and do not believe in them for whatever reason. As time goes on, however, families are working harder and harder each day to make ends meet, and they are learning how quickly all their accumulated earnings and wealth could dissipate. Some families are starting to learn about these planning techniques and want to use them. The bar is slowly understanding the trend and starting to come along, and they're understanding that how we used to practice years ago is not always the best way to move forward.

The question has always been whether attorneys are providing this advice to clients because of lack of knowledge or mindset. There is no doubt that the old-school attorneys learned estate planning the traditional way and are not aware of some of the newer techniques, such as the IPUG® Trust and allowing the grantor to be trustee. For many, it is certainly a lack of knowledge, but for some, even when they learn of it, it is difficult to accept these practices because they fly in the face of the rules that we learned in regard to tax planning. Traditionally, tax trusts do not allow the grantor to be the trustee because they include the money in the estate of the person creating it. Newer style trusts like the IPUG allow the grantor to be the trustee because most clients do not have near enough money to be concerned about the federal estate tax limit ($12.92 million as of 2023).

It is difficult for a tax attorney to come to grips with some of the techniques that are being taught on the elder law side simply because the rules are different, and the game is a far cry from what they know. We're not looking to get the money out of an estate, but rather keep it in the estate for the step-up in basis.

As time progresses, the mindsets are starting to shift. More people than ever know someone who lost a significant amount of assets to long-term care costs and do not want that to happen to them or to their families. However, if the clients who are pursuing this traditional estate planning need to do so, the truth is they will be left behind. The law provides for this type of planning. If people choose not to protect their assets since so many others do, they will be alone in losing their stuff to long-term care costs.

The biggest stumbling block for clients is financial advisors who are not well versed in asset protection. They certainly know and understand financial planning, tax planning, and growing wealth, but that does not mean that they know and understand asset protection. This unfamiliarity often leads advisors to unintentionally give bad advice as it relates to asset protection. The key is that all professionals are doing what the client wants and what the client's desires are. We need to explain all angles and allow the client to decide what is best for them and their families.

TO TRUST OR NOT TO TRUST AN ATTORNEY: KNOW YOUR OPTIONS AND DO THE RESEARCH

In response to Smidge's question of "Who do you expect to pay for your care then?" Bob replied, "I understand that there are programs available and that the federal laws do provide the option for families to be able to do asset protection."

Attorney Smidge, who was a small-town estate planning attorney in York, Pennsylvania, said, "Sorry, but that's the first I've heard of that, and from what I know, asset protection is impossible! The only way to qualify would be to spend down the money on the nursing home to get to the threshold amounts for Medicaid."

Bob looked at Sally and said, "I know that doesn't seem correct, but he's the expert, so I suppose we'll have to trust him." Little did Bob know he was wrong in thinking that. The reality is people can always seek a second opinion or do the research themselves.

Attorney Smidge asked, “Bob and Sally, is there anything else that you would like to accomplish?”

Bob replied, “Yes, I want to make sure that we keep the costs down as much as possible that we will owe to you, the attorney in probate, when we die.”

To Bob and Sally’s distaste, Attorney Smidge replied, “There’s really nothing you can do about that. It’s the cost of doing business, and it is what it is.” The attorney’s response was very off-putting to both Bob and Sally.

Again, Bob seemed confused and responded saying, “Okay, I understand, but please don’t forget that I want to make sure that our children are protected after we die.”

Attorney Smidge found this to be rather offensive and said, “Your job was to raise them, not to control from the grave.”

Bob replied assertively, “I do not want to control from the grave; I do want to protect from the grave.”

“Now that is your opinion. Truthfully, you do not have enough assets to justify complex planning, and therefore, an outright base plan is all that your family needs,” said Attorney Smidge.

Bob acquiesced and agreed to this, again, because he believed Attorney Smidge to be the professional, and went along as he set forth. In some ways, Bob was relieved that he only paid $250 and the documents were prepared and signed with the paralegal that same day. He felt that it was good to have at least something in place.

Chapter Two

Bob's Gut Feeling: Something Is Not Right

A ONE-WAY STREET: SEEKING LEGAL ADVICE

Approximately six years later, Bob Jones paid a visit to Attorney Smidge's office and indicated to him that his wife, Sally, was not doing well and had been suffering from dementia for about three years. Bob said to Attorney Smidge, "My wife is becoming very difficult to care for, and I know she will definitely need assistance with her long-term care in the future." He went on to ask Attorney Smidge, "Are there any options or alternatives to get care for my wife, Sally, in our home or in a nursing home?"

Attorney Smidge said, "Well, Bob, in order to qualify for Medicaid in the state of Pennsylvania—whether it is in the home or in the nursing home—the person who qualifies for benefits cannot have assets greater than $2,000, and the spouse can keep half of their assets but must spend down the other half on their loved one's care."

Bob was very uncomfortable with the advice that he was given because he had definitely heard that there were ways for spouses to qualify for long-term care benefits and for the other spouse—the community spouse (meaning the well spouse who was remaining at home)—to retain set assets. Bob asked yet another great question, "Now are you sure that those assets have to be spent down, and is there anything else that can be done about this?"

"I'm sorry, Bob, but unfortunately, the assets must be spent down and nothing else can be done," Attorney Smidge said. Bob's inner voice told him something was wrong with this situation; he didn't trust the response his current attorney had given him.

BOB'S CONCERNS WERE TOO GRAND FOR GOOD OLD ATTORNEY SMIDGE

Bob also expressed to Attorney Smidge that he was concerned about his own health. Bob said to him, "Let me remind you that it is undeniably my preference to be able to protect my three children's assets from divorces, nursing homes, car accidents, and other creditor or predator situations. I'll also ask you again if anything else can be done to protect my three children after my wife and I are gone?"

Attorney Smidge sighed at the question and said, "Once again Bob, it's not your job to control from the grave; plus remember you've raised your three children well enough to allow the curtain and the chips to fall where they may." Bob was put off by his attorney's response.

As a last-ditch effort, Bob reminded Attorney Smidge that he wanted to keep his costs down in probate. He didn't want the attorney to earn a substantial amount of the wealth that he intended to provide to his kids. He went on to ask Attorney Smidge, "Can you give me information about a revocable living trust or beneficiary designated assets?"

Attorney Smidge looked flushed with a bright red face. Clearly, he was frustrated and said, "I assure you I am doing everything I can to accomplish your goals, but unfortunately, I am unable to."

Bob thought to himself, does this guy know anything about the law or is he just too lazy to share the information with me? Bob's jaw dropped to the ground. You could see a look of disbelief on his face. Clearly, he was distraught. He couldn't believe that everything he'd worked for would be lost to long-term care costs for his wife and that when he was gone, his three children could lose the remainder through no fault of their own. To make matters worse, the attorney was going to get a substantial amount of a fee in probate. Bob realized that, on average, attorneys earn around 5% of probate assets to probate the estate. He couldn't understand or wrap his head around why there were no other options. He felt helpless and overwhelmed.

A SECOND OPINION

Bob decided to get a second opinion and was referred to another York estate planning attorney who came very highly recommended. When Bob entered Attorney Johnson's office, he immediately felt a similar vibe as he did with Attorney Smidge. The office felt very stuffy, and the team seemed bothered by them being there. Furthermore, he was charged to simply meet with the attorney before he could go into the conference room. Upon meeting Attorney Johnson, Bob was very clear of his goals, wishes, wants, and desires.

First, he wanted to know how to protect his lovely wife's assets from the nursing home and long-term care costs. Second, he wanted his estate plan to provide asset protection for his three children after he died. He wanted each of them to remain in control of the assets to the extent they could, but most importantly, not lose the money to a divorce, nursing home, or long-term care costs. Finally, he made it very clear to Attorney Johnson that he wanted options to avoid the attorney costs in probate.

Attorney Johnson sat for a moment to gather his thoughts. He did not want to offend Bob in any way. However, in his opinion, there was no way to protect assets from long-term care costs. The Medicaid laws were clear that you need to spend all the family's money above $2,000 on the nursing home, getting them to poverty levels, and then get the family qualified for skilled-level care in the nursing home. Attorney Johnson said to Bob, "There are no magic pills in order to qualify for long-term care Medicaid in the state of Pennsylvania, and the family assets must be spent down to the applicable limits." Period. End of story.

It felt like Bob had a déjà vu moment as this guy also sounded exactly like Attorney Smidge when he made a remark about wanting to protect the children. Attorney Johnson said, "Why do you want to control from the grave? You have raised your kids, and now it is time for them to spread their wings and prove that you raised them right!"

Bob tried to get a word in edgewise. He said, "Well, bad things happen to good people, and let me remind you that the current divorce rate is over 51%. And despite my love for my children in-law, I do not want them to get the money I worked my whole life to accumulate."

Attorney Johnson was snarky and replied with, "Bob, you do not have millions and millions of dollars. That type of planning is for the ultra-wealthy. You do not have enough to justify that cost." Attorney Johnson laughed under his breath as far as avoiding the attorney costs. He said, "There is no way to reduce the attorney fees. Probate is simply a cost of dying."

Bob simply did not feel like he got his answers. He felt somewhat defeated, and sick to his stomach. Yes, he got a second opinion, but he felt like the two attorneys were reading from the same script. No education. Just simple, direct answers of yes or no, and there was no discussion. It was the attorney's way of handling his situation, and that was that. How could these attorneys know what Bob wanted and what was best for his family? They didn't ask enough questions, nor did they care to. They simply wanted to finish with him so that they could move on to the next client. Dismayed and defeated, Bob gave up. As much as something didn't feel right, he was tired and worn out. He had no fight left in him and stopped after the second opinion.

SALLY TURNS UP IN THE NURSING HOME

While Bob and Attorney Johnson were meeting, Bob's wife was already in the hospital. Her doctors were communicating that Medicare would pick up the bill at the nursing home while she rehabilitated to get stronger and ideally go home. In the end, home wasn't an option. Fortunately, however, because she was admitted to the hospital for three days, she did in fact qualify for assistance with the rehabilitation bill—as it had been communicated. In fact, Medicare would pay for up to 100 days of rehabilitation.

The week after Bob's meeting with Attorney Johnson, she ended up in the local nursing home. Unfortunately, Sally had dementia. After 30 days of rehab in the nursing home, she refused care. She refused to go to rehabilitation. There is no way that she understood the consequence of not going. However, it did not matter. After the second time that she refused to go rehabilitation, the nursing home gave notice to Bob that as of Friday, she would be responsible for private pay and no longer qualified to have Medicare paying for her rehab.

Bob was shocked. They had a supplemental Medicare plan, so the co-pays were taken care of. Bob was going from paying absolutely nothing to having to pay the entire amount of $12,500 a month. Bob had heard that the average nursing home care costs in Pennsylvania was $14,000. Although the cost was less than he feared, it was still substantial and way more than he felt comfortable paying or could pay indefinitely.

Knowing that two lawyers told him nothing could be done, he felt utterly helpless and was totally living in fear. Bob realized that his wife had dementia. A person with dementia could live for years and years. Their minds deteriorated quickly, but their bodies could go on for a very long time. He did the math in his head ... $12,500 a month was approximately $150,000 a year. That was a half million lost in three short years, and she could need care for years to come. He wondered to himself how he would live and what would happen to his kids.

Bob found himself struggling with mixed emotions. On one hand, he wanted his wife to live forever. They'd had an amazing marriage that had been the envy of everyone they knew, and he wanted to be married forever. On the other hand, five years had gone by, and when Bob visited her at the nursing home, she did not even know who he was. She told him about her boyfriend at the nursing home. Bob was devastated. He knew that this was not her normal self that existed before all this happened. He knew that she had an illness, but that did not change the deep pain he felt when his wife did not even know who he was. Bob thought to himself, "How did this all turn out so poorly?"

He realized that until he got spent down to approximately $140,000, which was fast approaching, he needed to spend it down until Sally would qualify for Medicaid. He watched all the money that his family had worked hard for their entire life going out the window, and there was nothing that could be done. When he did visit his wife, she spent the entire time talking about her new boyfriend.

He was struggling inside and didn't know what to do. He didn't know where to go. The love of his life didn't know who he was, and pretty soon he would be spent down to poverty level. Bob was not sleeping. He felt that his world was caving in around him.

The world felt dark. Could he possibly want his wife to die? He watched the bank account dwindle each and every month and wondered how he would live on what was left.

As the day-to-day stress piled up on Bob, he was a shell of his former self. He felt empty inside as he visualized each and every conversation that he'd had with both Attorney Smidge and Attorney Johnson. Was it true that the law does not help people in his situation? Bob's heart told him that something was wrong. He genuinely felt that both attorneys were wrong. Maybe they weren't practicing law in the right practice area. Something seemed highly unethical. How could society let people go broke? How could there be no help? Was that right? Why had I thought Medicare would pay for our care for the rest of our lives? Countless questions were going through Bob's mind. There was no doubt that something unsound was happening with the way these attorneys were practicing law.

Chapter Three

Bittersweet Reality

THE THREE CHILDREN

Mark was a very responsible individual who was healthy and able-bodied and also had a full-time job. However, his marriage was not the best. He and his wife had often discussed whether it would be better for them to get a divorce.

James had Down syndrome (he had special needs), and if something were to happen to Bob and Sally, he would definitely require the assistance of a group home or other facility to help provide care. He did receive Supplemental Security Income (SSI) and Medicaid and would definitely continue to rely on those benefits in the future.

Kyle—the youngest of the three—had not yet fully developed into the adult that his parents had hoped for. He often made impulsive decisions and bought extravagant things, which made it unlikely that he would retain assets in the future. On three separate occasions, he'd lost all of his life savings to "get rich quick" business schemes that his friends had talked him into.

Attorney Smidge indicated to Bob that he understood the situation of the three children. He told Bob that the will that they'd created, providing the assets outright to the three children, was the type of planning that Bob needed and that he must trust him. The only recommendation he made in regard to James (who had Down syndrome) was to provide the money to Mark and allow him to take care of his sibling. The problem with this was that if Mark were to die, get divorced, have a stroke, or have a car accident, the assets wouldn't get to James. This was very risky planning, and ultimately Attorney Smidge convinced Bob to just leave the assets outright to James.

SPENDING DOWN THE ASSETS & LOSING SALLY

Fast-forward two more years where Sally had been in the nursing home for over five years, and they had spent down over $750,000 of assets on her care. Bob was starting to get very nervous because Attorney Smidge was not providing any guidance or steps as to how to move forward. He felt completely helpless as he was almost down to the wire for the applicable spend down amount. He was distraught. His health was failing. He'd saved his whole life to prevent this from happening. He knew that his wife's health was deteriorating, and it was time.

Time stood still as Bob got the dreaded phone call that his wife had passed. Although she'd been a shell of her former self and had not even recognized him, he was still devastated to have lost his wife. He'd known the day would come, but it just felt very surreal to him. His world had come crashing down once again.

TAKING CARE OF BUSINESS: ASSET DISTRIBUTION

Bob had a meeting scheduled the following week with Attorney Smidge to start filing the Medicaid application because he was now spent down to the correct limits. Unfortunately, his wife had died, and they could not file the application for Medicaid. The assets they'd spent were gone.

His wife had an account with a balance of about $2,000 and Bob had an account with $135,000. He also had his house that was worth about $350,000, a retirement account worth about $1 million, and life insurance of $500,000.

With a heavy heart, Bob went to see Attorney Smidge. He knew that it wouldn't be long before he would follow Sally to the grave. He was content and had lived a full and rewarding life, blessed with a lovely wife, children, and grandchildren. His wife was now at peace, and so was he.

When Bob and Attorney Smidge met, Bob was focused on the money that was about to transfer to his three kids. He realized that even though Sally had almost qualified for Medicaid, the house and his retirement, along with the life insurance policy, should be enough for his three kids to get to retirement. He asked Attorney Smidge again if anything could be done for his three children to protect the money but to no avail. Attorney Smidge's response was exactly the same, which was that Bob had raised the kids and should not control from the grave. At the end of the day, he was looking at each child getting $500,000 in assets.

Attorney Smidge taught Bob about the SECURE Act and how the three children must take money out of the retirement account and pay the taxes of their entire share in a ten-year period. However, each child could choose to take it in one year if they wanted. Bob was concerned that his kids would not be able to make those difficult decisions. He was not overly confident that Attorney Smidge would be a great resource for them.

He asked Attorney Smidge again what would stop his three kids from losing the money to their bad decisions, divorce, government programs, and so on. Attorney Smidge's response was, "You have raised your three kids, and now it is time for them to live their lives." Bob reminded Attorney Smidge that James was disabled and was receiving public benefits from the government. Bob swore he'd read something about special needs trust planning. Attorney Smidge scoffed and said that the planning they were doing would take care of it and for him to relax and trust the process.

Something did not seem right to Bob, but he figured the attorney was the professional. He continued to feel uncomfortable and pondered what to do. In the end, he decided to just take the professional advice from the attorney and give up.

BOB ROLLS OVER IN HIS GRAVE

Six months later, Bob passed away, and all the assets were distributed according to the last will and testament, which was outright to the three children. Mark was named as the executor in the will. Mark took the will and the paperwork and met with Attorney Smidge. Attorney Smidge explained the process of probate, including when the inheritance tax return was due and everything that Mark would have to do.

At the end of the meeting, Attorney Smidge told Mark that he was giving him a huge discount since his father had been such a good client and friend over the years. Attorney Smidge would invoice him a one-time charge that was 3% of the total assets, which amounted to $60,000. He explained that most attorneys would charge 5% and claimed he was saving them a ton of money. Mark knew that his father had trusted Attorney Smidge and had used only him for his entire life. He realized that even when his father had gotten a second opinion from Attorney Johnson, he still went back to Attorney Smidge. Little did he know the truth behind what his father dealt with during his time as Attorney Smidge's client.

Oblivious to the facts, Mark agreed to move forward and signed the fee agreement. As you can imagine, Bob was rolling over in his grave as he had not wanted the attorney to receive a large sum of the funds; his desire had been for the funds to go to his children! As you may recall, Bob had wanted protection of his assets for his children.

MARK'S INHERITANCE

Mark immediately took the money that he received from the inheritance and paid off the mortgage that was on his marital property. Mark got the opinion of his friend, who was a financial advisor, and learned that his decision was not a good one because he would have to liquidate his portion of the inherited IRA in one year and take all of the taxes in the same year. This meant that because he had liquidated the entire IRA in one year, he had to pay 100% of the taxes that were not paid during his father's life, all at once.

In Mark's mind, it was free money. He'd hated that he and his wife had a mortgage and had wished there was a way to get rid of the $500,000 mortgage. He'd believed that their lives would be so much better if he could just pay this off. The stress would be so much less if they didn't have the mortgage hanging over their heads. Their marriage wasn't the best, but he attributed that to the fact that their mortgage made them cash-poor. He resented his wife because he had not wanted a house that big. He didn't need something that huge or showy. The strain on their marriage had been palpable. Mark had decided to salvage his marriage. So, to take the strain off it, he would take the consequences on the IRA. This meant he was going to take 100% of the money to pay down the mortgage along with his small savings.

Mark came home a week later with a paper in his hand to show to his wife. (The paper was a mortgage satisfaction piece because he'd paid off the entire mortgage. She thought it was divorce papers.) At first, she couldn't believe that he was going to file for divorce before she even got the chance to do it. She'd thought for sure he was still in love with her and that she was the one who was going to break his heart. She'd met with her attorney a few weeks prior to discuss filing for divorce. The attorney had advised the wife of the laws in Pennsylvania. If Mark kept the inheritance separate, there really wasn't much she could do to get it. However, if Mark used it to pay down a marital debt, she would be able to keep half.

She knew her husband never got good advice from anybody. She'd always felt Attorney Smidge was getting quite old and was no longer on top of the laws. She also knew that unless Mark went to a divorce attorney, there wasn't anyone else in his life who understood divorce laws and everything else. All of this was swirling through her head. This was unbelievable! She couldn't believe he was filing for divorce.

She looked at the paper and realized it was a mortgage satisfaction piece. She realized that he had paid off the mortgage using the money from his father's estate and the little savings he had. He explained to her that he wanted the house to not be an issue and wanted them to start over. He apologized for the last few years and professed his love for her. He wanted to make their marriage work with all his heart. Now, with the mortgage no longer being an issue, there was nothing stopping them. Well, at least in his mind.

His wife didn't know how to react. Her dreams had just come true. She could now file for divorce and keep half of the value of everything, since there was zero debt in the marriage. She couldn't believe it was this easy. She decided to play it cool for the time being, but in her mind, it was over. It was also too late for counseling, and the mortgage was a small piece of the issue. Her new boyfriend whom she'd recently started seeing was the straw that broke the camel's back. Both Mark and his wife left the conversation agreeing to see how things played out.

A month later, his wife filed for divorce, and as part of the divorce proceedings, she ended up taking half of the value of the marital property. The significance of this is that, because

Mark had taken an inheritance and paid off a marital asset, his wife was entitled to half of those assets in the divorce. Therefore, she'd taken half of the value of the house that they owned. Mark couldn't believe what had happened. He felt cheated, like he'd lost everything! He hadn't hired an attorney before he'd made decisions about the money. By the time he'd gotten representation, all of the money was already liquidated and used to pay down the mortgage. He'd believed that he'd done the right thing. But at the same time, he felt like a fool. How was it that he was now divorced? Could this be real?

Essentially, the only asset they'd owned was the house that he'd paid for, and now he had about $200,000 owing after the legal fees. He knew his father would not be happy; he could see his father shaking his head at him from his grave. Mark sadly felt like he'd failed his father. The only good news was that if his parents had left everything outright to Mark, James would be without any money or access to it.

JAMES

Here you can say Smidge gave crappy advice again because he didn't explain how a beneficiary designation worked, and Bob had left his IRA going to all three kids. At least James got something! James received a notice, a month after his parents had passed away, that he would no longer be able to receive public benefits from the government. The problem was that he'd received money outright pursuant to the last will and testament, and he was receiving government benefits from the state of Pennsylvania. Therefore, he would lose his benefits and would be forced to go through the application process and spend down process in the future.

James contacted Attorney Smidge with the paperwork he'd received and showed him that he was losing his benefits. Attorney Smidge proceeded to tell him that the letter was correct. Since he'd gone over the resource amount of $2,000, he would lose his benefits, but once he spent the money down, they could reapply. James required significant assistance (he received Medicaid and SSI), and within the year, the assets were spent down, and the inheritance was gone.

James went back to Attorney Smidge, who filed a new Medicaid application and got approval for benefits. However, all of the money provided from his dad was gone. Again, not the outcome Dad had been hoping for. Dad had had greater hopes in protecting his children, and all his wishes were fading away into thin air.

KYLE

Kyle received the money and immediately went on a binge and a shopping spree and purchased frivolous items. Within one year, he ultimately spent all of the inheritance that he'd received from his parents. No, he was not disabled. No, he was not getting a divorce. No, he didn't do drugs or drink any alcohol. The son was simply not mature enough to handle receiving close to $500,000. He did not have to earn the money and didn't think much about it. He did not respect it because it was not earned through any hard work of his own. However, the bottom line was that it was gone. There was nothing left to show for it except a few trinkets that he'd purchased. The new car was probably his most practical purchase, even if he spent over $100,000 on it. Surely, his father was rolling over in his grave!

A CHANGE OF HEART

Mark entered Attorney Smidge's office fuming with anger and frustration. He reminded Attorney Smidge of exactly what his parents, Bob and Sally, had hoped to accomplish by using his services. He assertively told him that his parents' wishes were to protect their assets during their lifetime for them both, as well as have the assets protected after death, so that only the three children could enjoy and use the assets. Mark allowed Attorney Smidge to explain his position and knowledge, as well as his mindset in regard to the situation. Attorney Smidge reiterated what he'd told Mark's father repeatedly, which was that he didn't have enough money to do trusts and that it was not his job to control from the grave.

When Attorney Smidge was done speaking, Mark informed him of the fact that $750,000 had been lost to Sally's nursing home, and each child had lost all of their inheritance money (or at least half, in his own situation). He also went on to explain to Attorney Smidge what had happened with his wife and paying off the marital property, as well as how his brother had lost his government benefits and how his youngest sibling had recklessly spent all of his money.

Attorney Smidge replied dishonestly, "That is what your mom and dad wanted, and they did not want to control from the grave." Mark absolutely knew that that was not the case and reminded Attorney Smidge that he was in several of those meetings, and his parents' goal had been to protect assets during life as well as after death. Attorney Smidge said, "There was no way to do that for the modest means that Bob and Sally had; the plan that I used was certainly the correct plan, and I stand by that."

At this point, Mark realized that over $2.5 million of the family's money was gone. There was nothing that could be done. Not only did the parents lose significant wealth to a nursing home during their mother's lifetime that they did not need to lose, but the three children also lost their inheritances, through no fault of their own—simply because the planning was not done properly.

Mark now wanted to get a second opinion, but he realized it wouldn't matter. It was too late, and the money was gone. There was nothing that could be done. In that moment, Mark promised his dad that he wouldn't let that happen to his own family.

He decided to get proper counsel to ensure that his family was protected from his long-term care costs. Mark did some research on his own and realized he'd been given bad advice. Armed with that information, he was willing to pay for better counsel and get the right answers to protect his family. He would also safeguard his own children from any divorces and poor decisions, as well as protect their rights to government benefits.

PART II

Modern Solutions (Revocable and Irrevocable Trusts)

Chapter Four

Discovering Ultramodern Plans

SEEKING PROTECTION

Mark was now remarried and had three children of his own. He and his wife wanted proper planning to be done, and although his family had worked with Attorney Smidge, Mark questioned if proper advice had been given and whether anything else could be done. It was very important to Mark that neither he nor his wife lose significant wealth in the event that either of them were to need long-term care during their lifetime. It was also a priority for their three children to be able to keep their inheritances protected for themselves as a gift from their parents.

ESTATE PLANNING WORKSHOP

Mark saw a Facebook ad for the law firm of Bellomo & Associates inviting him to an upcoming workshop on estate planning and elder law called The Three Lands to Protect Your Family and Their Security. Mark talked to his wife and they pleasantly agreed to go to the two-hour workshop in order to learn more about not only the firm but also different planning techniques, and whether Mark had been correct this whole time (along with his father, Bob) about planning that could be done. Mark and his wife absolutely loved the two-hour workshop, as they learned that their father, Bob, and Mark were in fact correct—assets could be protected during lifetime, as well as after death.

He was eager to learn more about the specifics of the situation, as the law firm disclosed their fees during the workshop. He now understood what the cost would be for doing the planning that he was looking for. He and his wife agreed that they would like to attend the free consultation with the law firm called *a vision meeting*.

VISION MEETING

The first thing they noticed was how relaxed the atmosphere in the office was and how friendly everyone was. During the vision meeting, I entered the room and introduced myself. I asked Mark and his wife, "What brings you in today and what were you hoping to accomplish?" I could see his eyes light up and immediately, Mark said, "I want to protect my assets during my lifetime from the nursing home, and I want what happened to my parents, losing several hundred thousand dollars, to not happen to my wife and me. Also, any inheritances that our three kids would receive needs to be protected for the kids and only the kids." I was impressed that he knew exactly what he wanted and rightfully so!

I immediately wrote down exactly what the goals were on our client Goal Focuser™ sheet. I then went through the yellow information sheet that he filled out to get to know the family and gather more information about the situation. It became very clear from reading the yellow information sheet that the family rated asset protection during life from nursing homes and long-term care costs as the number one most important thing. The second-most important thing was learning more about protecting assets after death for the three children.

VISION CLARIFIER

Once we were done reviewing the yellow information sheet, I pulled out what we call the *vision clarifier*. This allowed us to take what the client told us about *what is important*, not only in their own words at the beginning of the meeting but also on the yellow information sheet, and bring it into our world with all possible plans that we would be able to do. I walked the family through the *vision clarifier*, explaining each and every plan that the firm offered. I also took them through all the costs associated with the plans, which mirrored the costs that were presented in the workshop.

Mark immediately commented, "Yes, those were the prices that you said the other day, so at least that matches." We all had a chuckle, and I left the *vision clarifier* on the table. These were my kind of clients—very personable with a great sense of humor!

I said to them, "Please take as much time as you like to determine what plan you would like to go with, and if you'd like me to leave the room, I would be more than happy to."

A SPEEDY DECISION

Mark immediately responded and said, "No, we don't need any time; we know exactly what we want. This is what we have been looking for, for years, and my parents' unreliable attorney said that nothing could be done. Thank goodness we found your law firm, as your plans are just what we need." We then agreed to enter into a signed engagement agreement, which authorized the firm to begin the asset protection planning for the family. Mark and his wife were so impressed by how much time the team spent with them teaching them the plans. They knew what they wanted and what was best for their family. That was better than relying on the word of an attorney like Attorney Smidge, who thought he knew what was best for the family, even though he barely knew them.

He and his wife came back approximately two weeks later and were given a *design meeting consideration checklist* to help them think about all the questions that they were going to be asked in the design meeting and be prepared to make it go seamlessly. Some of the questions they needed to carefully consider were what to name the trust and who should be in control (the trustee). Also, who they wanted to name as their financial and medical powers of attorney, as well as who the beneficiaries were and how they wanted them to receive the money. The family prepared in detail, and therefore, the meeting itself lasted only about 45 minutes.

At the end of the meeting, the family asked some basic questions and ultimately were excited for the documents to be drafted, which were signed and executed approximately two weeks later. They were impressed by the client service we offered and expressed to me how pleased they were. Nothing makes me happier than to hear a happy client's positive feedback!

We had a funding meeting about two weeks later, after the initial signing meeting, to determine exactly what assets were going to be put into the trust. I completed a funding chart indicating exactly what assets would be going into the trust, and what assets would be remaining outside the trust and staying in their name but would not be protected from creditors or long-term care costs. In this specific situation, we put in the trust several hundred thousand dollars of nonqualified assets (assets that are not retirement assets such as 401(k), IRA, 403(b), and so on, because these assets cannot go into a trust without triggering all of the taxes), as well as the primary residence and a cabin in the woods and a small beach property in another state.

These were the assets that we were looking to protect during their lifetime, and all their other assets would ultimately end up being protected for the three kids after the death of both of their parents.

WORKING OUT THE KINKS WITH THE RETIREMENT ACCOUNT

The one asset that proved to be difficult, that we spent a lot of time planning for and a lot of time working with other professionals on, was the million-dollar retirement account that Mark was able to accumulate. It was very important to him to protect the retirement money from any long-term care costs. However, in the state of Pennsylvania, if a person enters a nursing home and if their spouse wants to be able to protect a retirement account of the individual receiving care, we must liquidate the asset and then do other types of crisis planning to protect the money. Although it is doable, most individuals are reluctant to liquidate retirement accounts and pay tax consequences as well as potential Medicare Part B premium increases. Medicare Part B premiums are based on how much income a person has in one year. When a person liquidates a retirement account, it is treated as ordinary income and will raise the amount of money a person pays the following year for Part B benefits under Medicare.

I met with Mark's financial advisor and accountant to explain the situation, including what had also occurred to Mark previously with his father and mother and three siblings. It was very clear that Mark wanted these assets to be protected, but we all agreed that we needed to be very careful with how we went about doing it since he just recently turned 59 ½ years old and is fairly young overall. This means that we should have several years to stretch out the tax and should not have to pay it all in one year.

Ultimately, the three professionals agreed that it would be best to implement a five-to-seven-year plan for liquidating the retirement account, and each year we would pull that piece of the money out and pay the taxes on it, which would, according to our calculations, keep us under any major Medicare Part B premium increases. This is done so that a person does not pay too much tax in one year and to keep the amount they will pay for Medicare Part B in the following year relatively under control.

Once the money was liquidated and taxes were withheld, the remaining money would then be placed into the asset protection trust with the financial advisor using whatever investment tool or product that they deem to be the most suitable. We explained to the family that because it would take us five to seven years to get 100% of the money out of the retirement asset, there would still be an additional five-year waiting period until 100% of it was protected. This is because of the five-year look-back period for Medicaid purposes. Based upon the age and health of Mark and his wife, that was certainly a risk that they were willing to take and felt very comfortable to do so. Due to the fact that they were so young, they felt that their chances of staying out of a nursing home for five years was a good bet. We all agreed that we would continue to evaluate the retirement issue at the end of each year when we had the information available for us.

The retirement asset was not something that was an issue until the last couple of years when the SECURE Act came into existence. The SECURE Act provides the provision, among other things, that when a child inherits a retirement account from their parents, they have a ten-year period to realize 100% of the tax consequences. One exception to this rule is if the money is being paid into a special needs trust, in which case the money would be allowed to remain in the trust (accumulation trust) but also not be forced out in a ten-year period.

Since we were doing a special needs trust for their middle child, this was significant because we would be able to stretch the tax consequence out over the special needs child's life expectancy. We also discussed with a professional team whether we should change allocations based upon the fact that we are able to stretch that out. The SECURE Act allows a disabled beneficiary to pay the tax on the retirement account over their life expectancy. So, we discussed whether it would make sense to allocate more of the retirement assets to the special needs child since we could stretch it out to a special needs trust and the other children would have to cash it out over a ten-year period. Ultimately, we decided that was not necessary in this specific case.

ASSET PROTECTION TRUSTS

We agreed that creating asset protection trusts after death for the children would be the best way to preserve the money for the next generation. Each of the three kids presents a very different scenario which would be handled differently, based upon the specific facts of each case.

Dan seemed to be a responsible adult in his mid- to late-30s, with a very good head on his shoulders. He did occasionally have issues with his wife, and they had discussed whether it would be better for them to get divorced in the future, but they certainly had no plans to do so in the near future, and they were hopeful that they'd be able to work it out and be together forever.

Jeff had a disability and was receiving public benefits and would definitely need to continue receiving these benefits if something were to happen to his parents.

Reese had made some questionable decisions during his lifetime, and Mark was fearful that his youngest child would make more poor decisions and lose everything that he inherited.

Chapter Five

Next-Level Planning with Purpose

Planning is bringing the future into the present so that you can do something about it now.

—Alan Lakein

ESTATE PLANNING

I've certainly become modernized and have come a long way in the last 20 years. Attorneys often receive propaganda about different companies and organizations that can help them to grow their businesses and their practices. It is very hard when you are starting out to distinguish between the good and the bad companies and which ones are just good at marketing. It is tough to evaluate these companies and to tell which ones are actually legit and figure out the ones that won't be around in a few years.

When I ventured off on my own in 2009, I came across an organization called Lawyers with Purpose (LWP) and its founder, David J. Zumpano. The organization had the *educate first* mindset that I wanted to implement in my practice so that what happened to my family in the hospital room would not happen to any other family. They also shared all of my core values (see the foreword from David Zumpano where he lays out the LWP® core values and how I emulate them in my life each and every day). I have been a member of the organization since 2009 and have implemented their strategies, to the benefit of my clients, protecting millions and millions of dollars for their families. I would not be where I am today without this organization. I truly believe that the cutting-edge planning that we use and have used for 30 years is unmatched in the industry. The trusts and concepts that I will reference are all trademarked principles and concepts of Lawyers with Purpose®—I use them in this book with permission of the owner and founder, David J. Zumpano.

ANCIENT ESTATE PLANNING

Estate planning in 2022 is very different than it was in the late '90s. The landscape is different for a number of reasons. This is because of the following:

- The federal estate tax limit has gone way up (currently it is $12.92 million per person).
- We use trusts defensively: for example, when someone has special needs, is a spendthrift, or is in a bad marriage.
- We're also learning how to use trusts offensively: we will use trusts for people who are good with money, in good marriages, and in good health.

Overall, we want to make sure not to lose the money in case something bad happens to a good person.

The attorneys practicing in small towns across the United States often have difficulty paying for a national company that stays on top of the law and provides software that gets updated on a regular basis. The pricing structure has certainly changed over the years, but when I joined the organization, I had to take the last $20,000 on my line of credit to get my team trained and to get access to the software. I still say that was the best investment I have ever made in myself and in my firm.

The firms I worked for previously used the same form for years and years. Oftentimes, the same spelling mistakes are still in the documents that I review, which come from these firms. That was simply how it was done with good old attorneys like Attorney Smidge and Attorney Johnson. They were taught estate planning by their fathers who were attorneys, and that's just how some of these traditional attorneys learned time and time again. They know how to practice law and do not need some national company barking orders at them to do this or that, nor do they want to use the documents that they didn't write themselves.

THE MODERNIZATION OF FORMS, PLANNING TECHNIQUES, AND CONTINUING LEGAL EDUCATION

The Lawyers with Purpose documents get updated about three to four times a year. Each update is generally due to a change in the law or a change in the Program Operational Manual Systems (POMS) or changes in case law. The biggest area where change seems to affect documents is in the special needs planning area. This area changes often because of the fluctuations in both the Social Security Program Operational Manual Systems (POMS) and the *Medicaid and Long Term Care Handbook* in Pennsylvania, or even changing regulations. I recently looked at a special needs trust from an attorney I respect and adore. The form was from 1994, and it was still the same form he used the day he retired in 2021. It is hard for me to fathom that the same form was used and never updated from 1994. Clearly, some firms are still stuck in the Stone Age, and implementing modern practices, including updating a form, just hasn't crossed their minds. They have more important matters to deal with, right? Or are they simply so entrenched in their ways that doing it another way never crosses their mind?

Similarly, planning techniques are often changing, but many attorneys do not even know it because they stay in their offices, unwilling to pay to travel across the country to learn from the top experts in the field. The continuing legal education (CLE) that we attend can be in any practice area, and many attorneys simply take what they can get to meet the basic requirement. Furthermore, to the extent that they do attend a session relevant to their specific practice area, most attorneys who teach the relevant CLEs do not want to give too much away to their competitors, so they keep it close to the vest. They won't divulge pertinent information that is of much substance, and therefore, it is generally a waste of time for the person attending. It's a sad fact, I know, but it's the reality of what goes on in the industry.

NATIONAL ORGANIZATIONS

There are numerous national organizations that purport to help lawyers grow their practices and teach them what they need to know to be successful. I luckily found Lawyers with Purpose (LWP), which shares my core values and makes me a better person and attorney. I am sure there are other people who have dealt with the same organization who that would resonate with. I was a member of two other national organizations to see what they had to offer. But for me, there is nothing that can change your life and your practice in the same way that LWP® can.

However, the point isn't about the specific organization but the fact that the laws and techniques are changing way too fast so that it becomes risky not to belong to an organization that updates you on a regular basis. Yes, these organizations can be expensive, but they are well worth it, and they force you to travel several times a year to attend their meetings (to learn from them and continue to implement their systems and processes) to get outside of your own bubble and essentially learn about the changes and the new ways to practice law, not to mention changes in the law and how to stay up to date with them. I could not imagine doing it any other way.

CUTTING-EDGE PLANNING

Bellomo and Associates prides itself on its cutting-edge planning to get our clients the results they are seeking. We believe in giving clients a way to provide asset protection during life using an irrevocable grantor trust (this is a trust that is still in the grantor's Social Security number and allows the grantor to be the trustee) for asset protection purposes. We also plan for families to be able to protect from the grave using separate share trusts for each child and/or beneficiary. This allows the beneficiary to receive the money fully protected from long-term care costs. We also offer special needs trust planning, which allows an inheritance to go to the individual receiving benefits without losing their benefits and still have access to the inheritance through the use of a trustee. All this is a picture-perfect scenario that had Bob wanted for his plans! Luckily, his first-born child had the courage to seek out these modernized plans himself. Bob's wishes didn't come undone, after all.

MAINTENANCE FAMILY PROGRAM

One of the biggest things that we focus on is our maintenance family—a.k.a. the Red Wagon Club. To be a part of this, our clients can choose to pay a small fee per year (to stay in our program), and they will have the opportunity to come into our office to get updates about law changes and have access to other information to ensure their plan will work when they need it. They also receive invitations to monthly events throughout the year. The program allows them access to monthly speakers. We recently had our social worker talk about life care planning and how to know when a loved one may need more care. And another speaker talked about real estate and what to do when you need to downsize and what to look out for. Clients also get one year's worth of maintenance meetings (usually held once a month). It allows our families to come in as often as they can because they are paying between $395 and $795 a year. The hourly rate for our attorneys is $400. Having the ability to maintain this relationship with our clients ensures that they continue to enjoy the most important part of their plan: peace of mind when it comes to their family's security. We also give deep discounts on future services for our Maintenance family members.

REVOCABLE TRUST

We use a revocable trust in instances where people want probate avoidance because they own property in different states or when they want asset protection after death. A person must go through probate for assets that they own in their name alone. If a person owns property in three states, they will be forced to hire a lawyer and go through probate in every state where they own property in their name alone. The asset protection trust that we use is an IPUG® trust (a trust trademarked by David Zumpano and Lawyers with Purpose). It is a grantor trust that is irrevocable. It allows the grantor (the person who creates the trust) to be the trustee (the person in control) as well as the grantor. It is still included in the grantor's estate, so the children get a step-up in basis when they sell the asset. We used to be able to use a will that has a testamentary trust in it.

Over the last six months, we are now up to over seven companies who will flat out refuse to change the beneficiary to the trust. Now, we are using revocable trusts, which also provides a benefit to our families since there is a 2% fee for revocable trusts on death. This is currently the only way that we can get around the refusal by these companies to allow us to name a testamentary trust as a beneficiary. The maintenance family members get deep discounts for trust administration. The aim here is to essentially avoid those massive fees in a will.

This is something Bob would've loved to have done in his will. Remember how he was so insistent on not having to pay a large fee to Attorney Smidge? He wanted his hard-earned money to be protected from paying hefty legal fees. But as you can recall, Attorney Smidge said there was no way around the fees. He even told Mark a lie that he was giving him a discount on the fees, but he still charged him a large sum of $60,000, which was 3% of the total assets. Imagine how happy Bob would be today if he had access to these modernized plans!

Chapter Six

Send Clients Home Happy: How Trusts Work

RADIO FLYER RED WAGON

During the workshop, it was very clear that Mark loved learning about the Radio Flyer Red Wagon (remember from childhood, everyone had a Radio Flyer Red Wagon or knew someone who did)—an easy and simple way to teach how trusts work. The red wagon is a concept that is a teaching tool used by Lawyers with Purpose. It was obvious during the workshop that the family was understanding and totally grasping the concept of the red wagon. Imagine that you are a child pulling a wagon behind you, and it's filled with your favorite things, like Barbie dolls, G.I. Joe figures, or rocks. And as a child, you are happily pulling this wagon with a sense of pride and security because you are in charge of keeping your belongings safe and close by. Similarly, as adults, we would want to have precious assets near us as well, such as our house, our money, and our properties.

We use little boxes and put them into the wagon to visually illustrate that the actual asset is now in the wagon for the benefit of the individuals. A good chunk of time is spent describing how you get asset protection during life. This happens by having the individual give up direct access to an asset and waiting five years for the look-back period to expire in order to be able to protect 100% of the assets.

DIRECT ACCESS ON A SILVER PLATTER?

We further teach in the workshop how an individual would be able to obtain money out of the trust if it was necessary—for example, for emergency purposes—through the use of a child or another trustworthy family member or friend. The mechanism to do this is for the person in control (the trustee) to write a check to the lifetime beneficiaries (usually the children), and then the children of their own free will write the check back to the parents or pay the bill on the parents' behalf.

During the workshop and the vision meaning, one of the first things Mark and his wife expressed was that not only did they want the assets to be protected for them and their children, but they also wanted a Radio Flyer Red Wagon to bring home. Why is this so? Because the concept of the Radio Flyer Red Wagon as well as protecting your family resonates with the family and many other families who we work with. The asset protection piece is the easy decision for most families. However, there are always going to be *assets that we will leave out in the name of the individual and not place into the trust* because *they want direct access* to it (the key is to allow the clients to live like they used to but at the same time getting asset protection). In most cases, we will use a revocable living trust because not only will that allow us to avoid probate during life (because we are using a trust, the assets will pass automatically to their loved ones and they will not have to go through probate) but also to do asset protection after death for the three children. We got down to business and designed a plan using a *revocable living trust* so that we would be able to protect the assets for the three children after the death of Mark and his wife.

THE FAMILY IS ON CLOUD NINE: PLAN IS SET

The family was ecstatic knowing that they had a plan in place that not only provided asset protection during life but also asset protection after death for each of the three children.

Before we jump into Dan's situation, let's summarize what a *revocable trust* is: it is a trust that the grantor or grantors (the people who created it) can change their minds about and take assets out of by themselves. An *irrevocable trust*, on the other hand, is one that provides asset protection because the grantors cannot take the assets out of the trust and give them directly back to themselves. For Dan, both the revocable and irrevocable trust poured into a separate share trust solely for him and allowed him to be the co-trustee with an individual of his choosing. He chose a close family member who was his cousin and happened to be around his age. He would be allowed to manage the money day-to-day and would only need his cousin to sign off if he would be pulling any amount of money out of the account that is owned by the trust. Because there is a co-trustee and he cannot directly access all of the money by himself, he will receive asset protection from creditors including his spouse.

The planning also provided for a special needs trust for the benefit of Jeff so that he would be able to inherit the money from his family but also continue to receive the benefits that he is still entitled to.

Reese was also protected in a way that only he would be able to access the money, but it would be protected from his creditors, predators, divorces, as well as his poor decision making. In this case, they appointed a friend who happens to be an accountant to be the trustee of the money for the benefit of Reese. They did not allow him to pick his trustee and certainly did not allow him to fire his co-trustee like they did for Dan. The person creating the trusts after death will make decisions like this based on the children and their lives. In a case like Dan's, he was responsible and was good with money, but Reese was not, and therefore, Reese did not have the freedom to fire the trustee. However, the money was protected because it did have an associated trustee and he was a professional, which gave us the benefit of the doubt that he would do things properly, and Reese would still be protected if the trustee did not.

The family was thrilled after the signing meeting. Now they had put into place what the office of Bellomo and Associates calls an *enhanced AP2*, which provides for a revocable trust and an irrevocable trust, along with after death separate share trusts for each child to allow them to keep their money protected (with them and only them) so it cannot be lost to any creditors whatsoever.

ATTORNEYS IN THE DARK SPARK DISAPPOINTMENT

Mark and his wife were overjoyed that this planning was available but also hurt and a little upset about the fact that it could have been done when his parents were doing their planning. Unfortunately, the attorney that his parents had worked with was not an attorney who was familiar with this type of planning and therefore was not able to do so. Mark asked me, "Is there anything that you could do in regard to Attorney Smidge?"

I replied, "Sadly, no, because he is an estate planning attorney and did not hold himself out as an elder law or asset protection attorney. This means there would not be liability on his part. It's an unfortunate situation, but the good news is your father would be so pleased with you setting the wheels in motion for protecting your own assets for your family."

I completely understood his frustration and that his family went to a professional expecting to have the money protected and was told it could not be done. This certainly serves as a disappointment for this family and many other families who are told something similar. But the somber truth was that the attorney just did not know how to protect the assets in life and after death, or how to set it up properly. Basically, his parents' attorney had been in the dark about ultramodern planning in elder law and asset protection. And clearly, more attorneys need continuing legal education to keep up with the needs of clients in the modern day.

Chapter Seven

Revocable Trust: Does It Work for You or Against You?

UNFINISHED BUSINESS: DOES THE TRUST TAKE EFFECT?

Revocable trusts have historically been used primarily as probate avoidance trusts (trusts that avoid the legal process that the state requires you to go through if you own assets in your name alone. Since these assets are owned by the trust, they do not have to go through the state process called probate). Prominent advisors and national speakers often talk about how everybody needs a revocable trust to avoid probate and save people's money from lawyers as well as costs to the state and county. At the beginning of my career, I worked for a law firm that assisted in getting several attorneys disbarred. These were attorneys who owned law firms that would hire insurance agents to go around preying on the elderly and coercing them into creating revocable trusts, under the disguise of protection. Little did these poor old folks know that they were being cheated.

They would put the revocable trust in a big, beautiful binder and hand it to the family. Then, two or three years later, the insurance agent would typically go back out to try to sell these elderly families products such as insurance and annuities, but they never finished or completed the funding process of the trust. This funding is when you change the ownership of the assets into the trust versus just leaving them in the person's name alone.

Families would have no idea that this funding process was not fully executed, until it was too late. They would learn of it when someone passed away. In some cases, they would even think that the trust they had in place did protect their assets. However, that was not the case. If a trust is not funded, then the asset is still left in the individual's name alone or however it was titled previously. Essentially, this means that the trust never takes effect or is never able to do anything because the assets are not owned by the trust. The trust is useless at that point.

To use the wagon analogy that we discussed earlier, the box never gets placed in the wagon if the titling of the account is not the trust itself or the wagon itself. In these cases, the trust never got funded, which means the trust did nothing. The asset was still owned in the person's name alone and therefore had to go through the probate process. If the asset was owned by the trust, then the trust would be the owner and avoid probate and the trust terms would control it. Therefore, many people were dying, and their appointed agents were realizing that the trust never did anything because there were no assets owned by the trust. Therefore, they had to go through probate and follow the instructions of the will anyway. In more egregious cases, family members swear that the insurance agent told them that this revocable trust would provide asset protection during life, only to find out when a loved one entered a nursing home that a revocable trust does not provide asset protection.

DIRECT ACCESS

If you think back to what provides asset protection—our creditor law always states that whatever you have *direct access* to, so too does the creditor. In instances where the creditor or the debtor has direct *access, so too does the creditor*. The bottom line of a revocable trust is that it is revoke-able and changeable—it can be revoked or nullified immediately by the grantor himself or herself. Because of that, there is no asset protection and there could not possibly be. However, it leaves unfair circumstances for the clients, as family members believed they were told that it would provide asset protection—sadly, the cold truth is that's not the case. Because I worked with this law firm in my early days and assisted people in getting disbarred, my personal feeling was that revocable trusts did not have an honorable place in estate planning.

CREATE SEPARATE SHARE TRUST IN THE WILL

This is a very unfortunate position because revocable trusts are extremely helpful and provide not only probate avoidance but also disability planning, and it's much easier to transfer assets automatically on death than to go through a probate process. However, because of my early experience as a young lawyer, I did not give revocable trusts a decent or fighting chance for most of my career. We were blessed during my career that we were able to use a last will and testament and create within the will a *separate share trust* after death for the benefit of the children. We would simply notify the company and change the beneficiary to the separate share trust for the benefit and overall protection of the child.

ROADBLOCKS

This worked for approximately 15 to 17 years, but unfortunately, in the last several months, we have been getting pushback from several large national companies that they will not allow us to name a beneficiary to a separate share trust. The only solution we've come up with is to avoid using testamentary trusts, and now we're using revocable trusts instead.

They have indicated to us on numerous cases that they wish that we would just use a revocable trust like every other attorney does. I have inquired numerous times to several individuals as to why this is even an issue, and I'm being told that it provides more security and less ability for people to commit fraud. The other reason is that they want the entity to be existing during life, whereas a testamentary trust, which is a trust that is created in the will, does not become active until death.

PROTECT FROM THE GRAVE

I honestly do not understand the distinction, but now that we are up to seven companies who refuse to do it, I am left no choice but to continue and to start to use *revocable living trusts* in order to be able to provide asset protection after death.

As a quick reminder, a revocable trust is a trust that allows the grantor (creator) to be the trustee (controller) and also pull the assets out of the trust by themselves, which does not give them asset protection but does allow them to protect the assets for their children after they die. Many families like the family in our story want to *protect from the grave* to ensure that only their children can receive the money—not the spouses or other unscrupulous individuals who may prey on their family members. This is a very common planning request within our firm, as people want to make sure that their children are protected, whether it be from spouses or nursing homes or car accidents or stupid decisions. Protecting from the grave is far better than controlling from the grave.

I have spoken to numerous other attorneys who are running into a very similar situation that we are in, and if a family wants to provide asset protection after death, they are left no choice but to do it within the revocable trust. Revocable trusts are going to become more common planning and more regular, and that is how attorneys will start to accomplish the objective of asset protection after death on a regular basis. Revocable trusts are the future of asset protection after death.

Chapter Eight

Irrevocable Asset Protection Trust During Life

CONSEQUENCES OF TRADITIONAL ESTATE PLANNING

Traditional estate planning has often used irrevocable trusts—most of these trusts that attorneys are accustomed to using are *traditional tax trusts*—meaning the money is outside of the estate of the grantor and does not count toward the estate tax calculations. For this to take effect, the grantor (creator) cannot be the trustee (controller) because we want the money in the trust not to count for federal estate tax purposes, nor can they have any incidents of ownership, actual ownership, or say over the assets. Furthermore, once the children receive the assets at death, they get a carryover basis (the basis that the grantor had when they put the asset in the trust because it was outside their control), which is the basis that the grantor originally had. So, when they go to sell houses or stocks, there is a likely chance that they will have huge capital gains consequences to this decision. This is a huge reason why people do not want to use non-grantor trusts, which are used for tax purposes where the grantor (creator) cannot be in control or have any say in what happens to the assets.

THE CONVERTED LANDSCAPE

Let's explore how the landscape of modern estate planning has changed with regards to the irrevocable trust. In a Law Review article, David J. Zumpano introduces the concept of an IPUG trust whereby *the grantor can be the trustee of an asset protection trust.* The ability to do this is the sole reason that the landscape in trust planning has changed completely. In the nearly 15 years since this Law Review article came out, thousands of lawyers across the country have been using this style of trust. Why? Because it allows for asset protection during the life of their clients and authorizes them to be the co-trustee of the money as well. We have been using this technique in our office for approximately 15 years, and clients love the flexibility that it provides, such as the following:

- Asset protection security
- Step-up in basis for the children to avoid the increased capital gains taxes
- Long-term care asset protection for the family

Most importantly it allows them to maintain control over their assets, even though they are owned by the trust. Fundamentally speaking, we do encourage the grantor to be the trustee of the trust, and because we are not trying to keep it outside of the estate tax realm, it is okay to allow the grantor to have control in that aspect. It is well settled in most states that this is not an issue, and, particularly in Pennsylvania, it's not a problem when planning for our clients.

THE FIDUCIARY OBLIGATION

Many clients whom we work with choose not to be the trustee of the trust because they have reached a point in their lives where they do not want the added stress of handling that portion, or they simply feel it is time to pass the torch onto one of their children. Either scenario will work. As Dave Zumpano explained to me, the courts expect that each fiduciary will act in the capacity of that role. For example, a person who is a trustee, but also the grantor, is deemed to be acting in two different capacities and has a fiduciary obligation in both. Furthermore, it is well settled that they will in fact act within their capacity of each independent role and will not cloud their judgment as to their position in other aspects of the trust, whether it be as the grantor, the trustee, or the beneficiary. We allow our clients to decide what makes the most sense for their families and act accordingly.

FIVE-YEAR WAITING PERIOD FOR LIFETIME ASSET PROTECTION

The irrevocable pure grantor trust, also known as the IPUG trust, encompasses asset protection during one's lifetime. Due to the five-year look-back in place under the Medicaid rules, it is essential that the assets be funded in the trust for at least five years and one day in order to receive 100% asset protection. This period is required because Medicaid has a five-year look-back period on all transfers. Transfers to a trust are subject to the look-back and do count as a gift for Medicaid purposes. We always discuss this with our clients, and in many cases, it serves as a reminder to people who are on the fence about whether they should move forward. That time is, in fact, of the essence, and five years is not guaranteed to anybody. Therefore, the best time to fund a trust is now while you are healthy. Waiting only increases the risk that you will not make it through the five-year look-back period, and the assets are therefore not protected.

AFTER-DEATH ASSET PROTECTION

Moving forward, we will be using revocable trusts as a mechanism to provide asset protection after death. In the upcoming section, we will discuss our ability to use *irrevocable trusts to plan for after-death asset protection*. This is another technique we often do because most families who want to protect assets during their lives are also interested in protecting them for their children after they are gone.

PART III

After-Death Asset Protection (How It All Comes Together)

Chapter Nine

The Family Wish Materializes

Every parent would be concerned if they knew their child's marriage was on the rocks and they had a high chance of getting divorced. Sadly, that's the case for Dan who is faced with the reality of divorce.

SEPARATE SHARE TRUST

In this instance, money that he inherited from his parents was not received outwardly by him but was rather placed into a separate share trust to be *protected for him*. It is often a very tough conversation to have with children because they are under the assumption that if a parent uses a trust, they, therefore, *do not trust them*. I'm not completely certain where this belief started or how it got its legs, but in most cases in my practice, when a child is there and I am speaking of trusts, I can see the disappointment written all over their faces, and it's a clear knee-jerk reaction to the circumstance at hand. The child's face either turns bright red and they refuse to make eye contact with the parents or the room becomes filled with an intense chill in the air.

"Now don't get me wrong, as I know that a separate share trust can sound like a trap to some people, but it's really not and here's why." I open up the dialogue to break the ice with the child. I go on speaking with reassurance to them in saying, "The truth of the matter is, you do have plenty of flexibility that goes into asset protection after death. This means that with the use of a separate share trust, you can still be a co-trustee and manage the day-to-day use of the account and investments; you'll really only need the other co-trustee to pull money out for you, and that person can do it in a blanket authorization." I start to see their faces light up and see them breathe a sigh of relief, and the common response that I get is, "Wow, that doesn't sound so bad, after all. I'm fine with that plan." The parents and I are pleased with the child's change of heart, as we can see that they are eager and agree to it pretty quickly!

APPOINT A CO-TRUSTEE

Obviously, if an individual is a spendthrift or not good with money, you would never give them *that type of control* that was just described. In cases where a person does need to be protected from themselves, you would *name a co-trustee* who your child must listen to in order to be able to take money out of the trust.

Reese never received the inheritance flat out. Why? Because he never got his money outright, he didn't have to make the decisions about what to do with the money. The fact that he was never given a choice ensures that he cannot make the wrong decision or receive bad advice. The money will always be made available for Reese for the remainder of his life, and his spouse will not be able to access it. Most particularly, he in no way had to make a decision about whether paying down the mortgage on the marital property would make sense or not. Sounds like a dream situation for someone that is undergoing divorce because all matters work in his favor, right? Some may think that this type of planning may be considered offensive to your in-laws. But very few people in my experience would expect it to be fair to receive that kind of windfall. If my spouse divorces me, then expect half of what we earned but not half of what my parents earned as well.

Sure, his brother is the co-trustee with him and yes, he did need to notify his brother and have his brother sign off on an authorization to be able to pull $50,000 from the account for a new vehicle. But it was well worth the phone call in exchange for knowing that money will be protected for the rest of his life—not only from his past divorce or future divorces, but also from long-term care costs and other creditors.

KEEPING THE MONEY IN THE FAMILY

Reese understood the importance, not only to his father but to his grandfather before him, of protecting the money that they've worked so hard for, for future generations. I will never forget the day when Reese thanked me. He said to me, "Jeffrey, I am truly grateful to you for protecting me from myself when I didn't even know I needed it."

I assured him, "Hey, it's my job to look out for clients, but I can't take credit, as that was your grandfather's influence on your father—it wasn't that they didn't love you or trust you, but the truth of the matter is that sometimes bad things can happen to good people—we simply just want to make sure that the money stays within the family."

SPECIAL NEEDS TRUST

As you may recall, Jeff had special needs. In a situation where there are special needs (in this context the most important issue is whether the person is receiving government benefits such as Supplemental Security Income (SSI) or Medicaid (Medical assistance) and outright receipt of the money would disqualify them from benefits) and a *special needs trust* is going to be used, we always recommend that it be a professional appointed as the trustee. The reason that we suggest this is because a professional is someone who understands the rules regarding the special needs trust and how to protect the money. We'll dive deep into why this is important in Chapter 10.

BOB'S WISH LIVES ON WITH THE NEXT GENERATION

In the example of the three grandchildren, based upon the way that we set up the plan for the family, the money is now available for each of the three children. The inheritance is not lost to the divorce (Dan), or to the government (Jeff), or to bad spending habits (Reese) but is available for each of the children to use as they see fit into the future. Surely, Grandfather Bob would be overjoyed to know his grandchildren had asset protection and were also blessed with security. Thanks to Bob's first-born child, his wishes and legacy lives on! He knew there was a way to protect assets in life and after death; and he was relieved to know there are attorneys out there who actually care to bring their clients' wishes to life.

CHAPTER TEN

THE DUTY TO PROTECT: SPECIAL NEEDS TRUSTS

It was a busy day at the office when my phone rang. I answered, and it was Mark's wife, who notified me of the passing of her husband. She was distraught. I expressed my deepest condolences to the family and assured the wife that I was here to ensure their plans were followed through in their will. She warned me that her second-born child was in a panic and was on his way to pay me a visit at the office.

WHAT HAPPENS TO MY GOVERNMENT BENEFITS NOW THAT FATHER IS GONE?

As I'd expected, Jeff came into my office in a frenzy after his father's passing. He said, "I'm very worried that I am going to lose my government benefits now that Dad is gone. What am I to do?"

First, I patted him on the shoulder, passing on my deepest sympathies for his loss and tried to comfort him with my words. "Your father was an amazing man, and please rest assured that he planned for the money to be placed into a *special needs trust* made especially for you. He went above and beyond in his planning to ensure you were taken care of. This means the money will not be touched, and you won't lose your benefits simply because you received an inheritance," I said to him. In this instance, Mark had provided the assets to Jeff in a special needs trust that had his brother Dan as the trustee of the trust. I could see the relief written all over his face.

"Thank goodness, Mr. Bellomo. All will be fine, after all. Thank you for providing me with a better understanding of what will happen with my inheritance and financial future. I'm glad my father picked you to be our family's attorney. Now I have peace of mind about my situation." He expressed this to me with deep gratitude. I was happy to give him assurance, especially during such a difficult time.

SPECIAL NEEDS TRUSTS

Special needs trusts were briefly introduced in the previous chapter, but here, we'll get into the details of why they are important. Third-party special needs trusts are trusts that are created by anyone other than the individual themselves, or in this case, Jeff. Because Jeff had never received the money outright, but rather his father had created it in his estate planning, the money was not subject to a look-back period (remember the Medicaid five-year look-back period?) and was immediately protected. Jeff would be able to receive government benefits for the rest of his life and not see any gap in coverage but also would continue to be able to receive the money through his brother as the trustee of the special needs trust (some people prefer family members to be trustees and others prefer professionals) when he needs it. This means that the individual could receive their money from the trust but also continue to maintain government benefits.

As you might recall, Jeff relied on these benefits, as he had special needs. There are some restrictions on special needs trusts that an individual must be aware of because you're only allowed to make distributions for the benefit of the beneficiary for things other than food and shelter.

The principle behind this rule is that the government benefits will be able to provide for the necessities of life, and the money in the special needs trust is there typically to enhance or supplement their life. The government will take care of the provisions of basic needs, and the other money will cover the frivolous or other expenses.

In Pennsylvania, it is imperative that the document specifically outlines the following detail: the trust itself is to supplement the benefit that an individual is receiving and not supplant the benefits. This means that the government does not want the trust to provide for the necessities of life because the government benefits are intended to do just that. Whereas the trust is used only to enhance a person's life.

In this instance, Mark had properly set up the distribution to Jeff, and he would be able to live his life getting his government benefits but also have open access to the money from his inheritance. However, it is worth noting that even if the money did go outright to the beneficiary who is on public benefits, we can still get them qualified for Medicaid and allow them to have access to the money. This mechanism is called a first-party special needs trust. The only downside is that they have payback provisions in them (they are also called D(4)A trusts). The state is entitled to get paid back up to the amount of money that they spent on the care for the individual. The problem is not many attorneys know about this and tell the person to simply get knocked off of benefits and spend all of the money down.

THIRD-PARTY TRUSTEES

In instances where siblings do not get along, or where the sibling doesn't want to have that responsibility for fear of a conflict arising with their sibling, the client does not want that sibling to be a co-trustee. We certainly recommend corporate or third-party trustees to act in this type of situation (e.g., companies such as Achieva Family Trust in Pittsburgh, Pennsylvania, that specializes in special needs trust planning). In particular, it is important to be very careful about who will be the trustee in an instance where there are government benefits involved, because if a distribution is made incorrectly, it could easily cause disqualification for Medicaid or Supplemental Security Income benefits.

The rules under the Social Security side are extremely complicated. Some of the obscure rules, such as the income deeming rules, make it virtually impossible to completely understand when they will deem something as income and reduce the benefit, or when they will not. When we are dealing with the special needs contact, my advice will always be to hire professionals who will act as the professional trustee. Why? Because not only do they fully understand the ins and outs of these trusts and implications, but they would also be bonded and insured in case of a mistake. There are a couple of Pennsylvania organizations that act as trustee in the special needs context; we often refer to them and have had wonderful results with their companies.

DUTIES AS THE TRUSTEE

In this particular case, we discussed the situation with the family. Dan was very confident that he understood the limitations in regard to the special needs landscape. But he also understood that he could contact a professional at any time and pay for their advice to ensure that he stays within his duties and fiduciary responsibilities as the trustee. Professional trustees know where the lines are, and they know how far they can go. In this scenario, Dan was comfortable with calling a professional because he was highly aware when he was "unsure" with regard to what he was doing. He chose to use them as a consultant rather than have them act as the trustee.

Chapter Eleven

Savvy Conversations to Secure & Protect

I had the lovely opportunity to walk the family through each trust individually. I explained to them how their separate share trust would work and why it was set up very carefully.

I'M CONFUSED ABOUT SEPARATE SHARE TRUSTS

Reese sat across the table from me in my office and appeared to be overexcited about receiving the inheritance that he had just learned would be passed onto him from his father. My personal feeling is that Reese was hoping that there wouldn't be a trust because (1) he assumed his dad wasn't worried about him getting divorced, (2) he wasn't even married, and (3) he was, indeed, a fairly responsible adult.

Here's how the conversation went in speaking to Reese. I said to him, "The assets have been placed into a *separate share trust* for your own benefit." I could see the look of disgust, confusion, and disappointment on his face. This was surely a moment of letdown. I spent a good amount of time explaining to him, "Now in having this trust created for you, your dad's intention was not to *protect you from yourself* but rather to *protect the money for you* to ensure financial security because his wish was for you to have this sense of security; he loved you dearly. This will allow you to have the freedom to do what you like for the rest of your life and not take any chances on outside influences or should anything else come up." He sat there silent, and I could tell it was taking quite some time for him to digest all this information.

HEAD IN THE SAND: TOUGH TIMES

Reese would occasionally drink too much. During those bouts of alcohol consumption, he would sometimes make poor decisions. Unfortunately, there was a period of time when he started to drink heavily and went on shopping sprees. He reached out to his brother (Dan) and said, "I need you to withdraw money from my trust for me. I need some cashflow right now." His brother was concerned and answered, "What do you need the money for now? I hope it's for something that is a necessity." He responded with, "What does it matter? The money is mine; just give it to me." Clearly, Dan was in an awkward position. He knew that something was wrong and that his brother was not acting normal. Dan went over to his brother's house and immediately noticed empty alcohol bottles scattered all around his floor and tables; he could smell alcohol on his sibling's breath. And knowing what had happened previously, he wanted to help his brother through this, so he sat down and had a heart-to-heart conversation. He went on to say, "I could tell you're going through a tough time right now, and I'm here to help you. You owe it to yourself to get cleaned up and not touch another ounce of alcohol. You don't want to repeat the same dark cycle you went through before. Once you're clean and have your life back on track, I will, of course, get you the money you need from your trust. But first, let's get you some help."

Reese felt better knowing his brother was there to support him, and he agreed it was time for a change. He was embarrassed but knew his brother was right and only wanted what was best for him. Dan was so thankful that their dad had had the foresight to plan ahead and make sure Reese didn't have direct access to the money; it just may have saved Reese's life.

THE MOMENT OF REALIZATION

The tension in the air during that period of his life was quite heavy. Reese, in hindsight, totally understood that the money was intended to be there for him and only him, and that it was not a way for his father to keep it from him but rather for him. He now had the strength to overcome this period in his life and still come out of it with all of the money from his father. In his own words, he expressed himself truthfully: "Had my father not done that for me, I would be broke and have absolutely nothing left, and for that I will be forever grateful." The two brothers were very close and would always remain tight because they appreciated each other, and when they were growing up, they were always there for each other, for moral support.

Dan understood that he was not trying to hurt his brother in any way, shape, or form but rather wanted to make sure that the money was there for him to use on things that he enjoyed, rather than wasteful stuff like spending sprees and alcohol.

FUTURE GENERATIONS BENEFIT

Although Mark was not alive to see what had occurred in all three situations, this was exactly what his father before him had been adamant about: protecting the assets for all his children in life and after death. He would have been very proud knowing that all of the money for the grandchildren that he left for the next generation was still available for his grandchildren and that to date, they had not lost any of it other than to valued purchases that led to a better life.

SHED THE STIGMA

It is very important to me that the stigma of trusts goes away. Trusts are not a negative word or an unfavorable tool, but rather they provide a positive outcome. *Remember, it is not about control; it is about protection when it comes to trusts.* In 20 years of practice, the one thing that I often see is that bad things happen to good people. In situations like that, assets could be lost quickly due to no fault of the individual. Had proper planning been done, that loss would have been avoidable and should be avoided. I'm hopeful that this book about asset protection and other books like it will make it more common for clients to use trusts.

We often run into issues with companies that do not completely understand how *to properly title a beneficiary designation*, or they simply want to do it their way. But at the end of the day, as time goes by, naming a trust as beneficiary will become more and more prevalent and easier to accomplish for people who are starting out in the field. I hope to make asset protection during life and after death more commonplace and easier for people to talk about. It is extremely rare for me to meet a family who does not want to provide asset protection for their children. Most families have a preference to ensure that only their children can receive the money and not outside influences. My job is to help families' wishes for asset protection become a reality that ensures security for their loved ones.

IGNORANCE IS NOT BLISS

Most people don't know that asset protection in life and after death is possible, and they are intrigued to learn more about the process. When that happens, I'm always open to showing and teaching families how to properly plan. And, as mentioned earlier on, we have programs in place to educate families about the modernized planning process. Remember in this case, *ignorance is not bliss,* and it's always better to be open to gaining more knowledge about using modern planning. The reason a lot of people don't do any planning is simply because they don't understand it. A confused mind says no. Once a client receives that education, it makes it easy for them to understand and to make decisions.

FIND THE GEM IN ESTATE PLANNING & MAKE IT MAINSTREAM

As time goes on, hopefully the stigma of trusts will dissipate as more people will utilize this type of planning to ensure protection of their assets. The increasing evidence of favorable results for clients, as discussed in this book and in my practice, definitely proves that the ultramodern planning techniques used in estate planning and elder law will absolutely become more mainstream now and into the future! I am hopeful that this book and its popularity will help advisors and accountants understand the importance of how trusts can be used and how helpful they can be for families.

Think about how many families will benefit from this type of planning and how pleased parents will be to have the ability to "Protect from the Grave."

Epilogue

As you know, the title of this book is *A Fork in the Road*, and it is essentially a metaphor for estate planning and elder law attorneys. Why? Because they take the road less traveled—the one that may be more difficult or more time-consuming, but ultimately in the end, they do what's best for the client and their families.

Mark experienced firsthand loss not only to a nursing home, but also after his parents died, when he lost a considerable amount of his inheritance to his divorce. This is because he decided to take the money and pay down the mortgage on the marital residence.

His siblings also lost out. Firstly, because James was receiving public benefits, and the plan was not put together correctly with the special needs trust, James lost his benefits and had to spend down all of the money and then reapply for benefits after everything was lost. Secondly, Kyle reached the age of majority, had access to the funds, and ended up blowing the money in no time at all. Mark saw how poorly his own affairs and his siblings' matters were handled and knew exactly what he didn't want to have happen with his own children, so he planned accordingly. Mark was able to protect assets during his lifetime from his long-term care costs, as well as to protect each of his children so that

100% of the money could be used for them and only them. That meant they would not lose any of their assets to a nursing home, car accident, divorce, or public benefits program.

Mark's own children learned the proper way to protect assets that they'd worked hard for during their lifetime, using the government's rules and doing exactly what they are allowed to do through the workshop and our process, as well as the use of the Radio Flyer Red Wagon. Then they passed that torch of wisdom on to their children to handle the assets in the same way. Mark's family was now armed with the tools to get the best of all worlds. As you can see, generations of this family were able to protect assets from long-term care costs as well, along with safeguarding significant wealth from attorneys' fees and probate administration. The end result was that ultimately, all assets after death were fully protected for their children and grandchildren.

To the attorneys who believe that a base plan is good enough, I urge you to please understand that we are the experts. We need to help people and listen to what they want. We need to remember that the law allows for this type of protection, and it is our duty to help families. And if you ask your clients what is important to them, 99% of the time, they're going to tell you that it's *protecting their legacy during their life and after their death for future generations*. Our job, as attorneys, is to do what the client asks—as long as it is within reason and within the law. There is absolutely no question that both are true here.

Please take the time to carefully plan for the future by using the tools discussed in this story to protect future generations. We are at *the fork in the road*. Although, we may have been forced to go down a particular road, in the end, it will be the *cream of the crop* in planning for the client. I hesitated and resisted this fork in the past, but now I understand that it is the best for all parties, including my clients, which is what was once lacking. Now, we will be able to do what our clients want, which *includes reduced costs* and *asset protection now and after death.*

The *time is now* to protect you and your family. Call the offices of Bellomo and Associates at (717) 845-5390 or check us out on the web at www.bellomoassociates.com.

Please attend one of our free estate planning workshops that will cover everything from A to Z on estate planning. In this workshop, you will gain valuable information, and you will learn what you need to know and what you need to look out for when planning. Also, you will learn how to protect assets during life and after death. It will give you everything you need to know about estate planning and elder law to be informed. Once you have attended one of our two-hour workshops, you will then be well equipped with the knowledge that is essential to protecting your assets in life and after death for your loved ones. Do what's right for your family and your hard-earned assets—you owe it to yourself!

Afterword

I was recently talking to one of my mentors and explaining the situation of what was occurring—how local institutions were not allowing us to name a testamentary trust as a beneficiary for asset protection after death. My mentor was curious as to why a base plan (base will, financial power of attorney, and medical power of attorney) giving everything outright to the children was not enough anymore. I explained that not only are there children who need to be protected from themselves, such as children with addictions or spending issues, but some who are special needs and are receiving benefits from the government. In a case like this, if the assets are in a special needs trust, the child can continue to receive the government benefits and keep the money from the inheritance. And if a special needs trust was not created, the child loses out on those benefits from the government. How, in that instance, would that special needs child be able to keep their head above water to meet their basic survival needs?

My mentor was clearly out of his league, not understanding the importance of the asset protection after death, because after all, "an outright will has been good enough for 45 years, so why is it not good enough anymore?" I also went on to explain to him that sometimes life does not turn out like we had hoped, and we want to have those assets protected—not from the child but *for the child.* His mind was completely blown by this statement, to which he was trying to be supportive and ultimately just said, "Well, Jeff, sometimes that's just the way the cookie crumbles, and you're just going to have to give the money outright."

In my heart and my soul, I believe wholeheartedly in the asset protection, not only during life but also after death. I have seen too many families lose their entire legacy and life savings, and I will not allow that to happen under my watch. The solution is simple: (1) a revocable trust for assets by which we're not looking for asset protection, but it will allow us to transfer the assets to the children; (2) assets protected after death including the Irrevocable Pure Grantor Trust, or IPUG trust, to protect the assets during life as well. I do not believe it's the way the cookie crumbles; I believe it's time for us as an industry to take the fork in the road that has been presented to us and not look back.

As I read the foreword by Dave Zumpano, his thoughts about me sharing his values and the core values of his company sparked a light bulb in my head—it dawned on me that those relationships with the professionals who we work with also share those values. As professionals, it is incumbent upon us to stay with the times to learn about innovative research and keep our eyes peeled for new opportunities that are available to us. It is not acceptable simply to say, "That is not how we did it in the past, or that is different from what I'm used to, so I don't want to learn it."

The core values that Dave lives by in his organization are to be open, curious, aware, collaborative, generous, and adaptable. As I was writing each chapter in this book, I realized that it's not only the professionals we deal with but also our very own clients who share in these values as well. Some attorneys are not willing to learn about the tools that can protect not only their clients but their very own families and future generations—they may not be open or curious, or they may not be aware or even adaptable—but they owe it to themselves to at least try.

My law firm shares very similar core values as those outlined by Dave. We worded our core values differently because the words that truly resonated with our firm are *how we live our lives, how we run our firm, and who we choose to associate with in our practice.* The bottom line is that as we move forward, it is critical for us to follow the rules and protect assets, not only during life but after death.

As I have always said, if the government doesn't like their own rules, they are the ones who can change them, and if they do (if the government does not want us protecting assets during life or after death, they are the ones who can change the law. It is our job as lawyers to carry out the law), we will certainly adapt and be collaborative to find another way to assist families with what is important to them.

To my fellow attorneys, *keep fighting the good fight. We are doing the right thing, and it is worth it.* To the attorneys who resist change, I implore you to be open, curious, aware, collaborative, generous, and adaptable from this day onward! Remember, we have the power to enforce real change for the good of the people. Our doors are open to you, so please don't hesitate to reach out. We're always happy to help guide and support you along the way. Let's continue to create a bright future for families like Bob's, as there's nothing more rewarding than seeing future generations shine!

Made in the USA
Monee, IL
04 November 2026

67384079R00059